D1391524

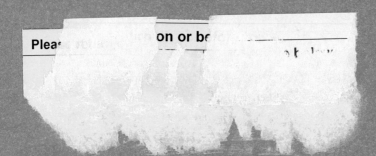

Please ~~re~~ **on or be** ~~t~~

Personal Best

Personal Best
Paul Floyd Blake

Dewi Lewis Publishing

■ ■ ■ ■ ■
impressionsgallery

The subtitle of a popular manual of sports photography, '*how to capture action and emotion*', spells out the principles of the genre.[1] Photography, with its ability to freeze motion, has been applied to sport since Eadweard Muybridge's human locomotion studies of the late nineteenth century. His photographic works such as *Man Walking and Throwing a Discus* (1887) perform both a scientific and artistic function, whereby the stopping of time is harnessed to enable technical analysis and aesthetic appreciation of the body in movement. The freezing of sporting action, enabling us to view at leisure dramatic moments that would otherwise pass in a blur, remains an important principle of the genre. We are all familiar with the stock shots: the sprinter thrusting across the finish line; the anguished face of the loser; the triumphant winner wrapped in a flag or brandishing a trophy. In this light, portraiture seems at odds with the essence of the genre. Sports portraits, where they do exist, invariably emphasise the sporting hero or celebrity, ranging from mass-produced Victorian *cartes de visites* of sports personalities, to today's glossy advertising campaigns that rely on famous faces – and bodies – to sell global sportswear or fragrance brands.[2]

The images of *Personal Best* are clearly far removed from either of these aspects of the sports photography canon. Paul Floyd Blake rejects the dramatic moment or celebrity portrait, instead choosing to make images of unknown athletes in quiet moments during training in anonymous sports centres. Working with a group of sixteen young people aged between 13 and 22, from different cultural and social backgrounds, and pursuing sports ranging from table tennis to taekwondo, Blake photographed them intermittently over a period of five years in the run-up to the London 2012 Olympic and Paralympic Games. His subjects almost always engage directly with the camera, acknowledging the presence of the photographer, and adopt simple or apparently artless poses. Sometimes the moment of preceding action is implied, visible in the wet footprints of swimmer Sophie Allen or the flushed face of long distance runner Rosie Edwards. In general however, these are images devoid of action. Rather, they emphasise the repetition and banality of training: the 5am sessions squeezed in before school, the chilly British mornings, and the bland institutional walls of the sports centre. These images pay tribute to the long slog towards glory that is not usually seen or celebrated.

As a youth, Blake himself was also a talented young sportsperson, spending evenings after school kicking a football around a North London car park, and eventually convincing the coach of Spurs to give him a three-day trial. Success in school and local semi-professional teams followed before social demands and lack of external support saw him drift away from the game. Perhaps this experience gives him an insight into the pressures faced by these adolescent Olympic and Paralympic hopefuls, whose training regime for selection requires both substantial financial and parental support, and a rejection of a 'normal' teenage social life. From the outset, Blake was adamant that he would carry on making portraits of his subjects, regardless of whether or not they were selected for Team GB and considered 'winners', or even continued in competitive sport. Throughout the process, he also encouraged them to keep notebooks or diaries, writing down their thoughts and feelings, selections of which now appear alongside their portraits. His approach emphasises a preoccupation with the individual's own story and motivation beyond the values and structures of competitive sport, as the title *Personal Best* suggests.

Blake's work has more affinity not with the canon of sports photography, but with that contemporary photographic approach to portraiture typified by uniformity and what Julian Stallabrass calls 'blankness'.[3] This strand of work, exemplified by Rineke Dijkstra, Thomas Ruff, Jitka Hanzlová, and Hellen van Meene, is characterised by a systematic technique in which subjects – usually individuals – are centrally placed within the frame and present themselves with the minimum of intervention of the photographer. The subjects may belong to a particular social group or demographic (adolescents are particularly prominent), and are generally portrayed in a moment of inactivity where their ambiguous gaze directly meets the camera. Stallabrass traces this approach back to nineteenth-century colonial ethnographic photography, in which exoticised 'types' are presented in a regular format characterised by the measuring stick and grid, enabling equivalence and comparison between subjects. In the contemporary manifestation of the approach, the subjects may not be so strongly differentiated from the viewer, but are similarly offered up for our gaze in an 'objective' manner, via large-scale, well-illuminated, highly detailed images that invite comparison and scrutiny.

Personal Best has some parallels with this approach. The young people were unknown to Blake, and were found at random via the third-party assistance of the charity SportsAid. He generally employs three compositional formats (close-up, head-to-waist, and full length), with a centrally placed figure returning the camera's gaze. This regular approach enables comparison across sports, inviting us to compare, for instance, the greyhound leanness of high-jumper Matt Roberts with the stocky strength of judo competitor Brandon Tuthill. Each sporting setting produces its own particular palette or atmosphere: pared-back whites, pewters and blues predominate in the fencing images; whilst in the track and field events, sportswear brights clash with muted English woodland hues.

More revealingly, Blake's long-term project enables comparison across time. A number of athletes decide, for one reason or another, not to pursue a competitive sporting career, and are subsequently photographed in their home environments whilst their cohort remain depicted in sporting settings. Bodily changes are tracked, prompted by training or injury, as well as adolescent development. Jawlines and cheekbones become more pronounced; puppy fat is lost and features become more angular; muscles are honed and skin becomes peppered with pimples. This kind of time-lapse device is perhaps not so far removed in essence from Muybridge's split-second motion studies, in that it makes visible and records those changes that would otherwise be imperceptible.

Blake's time-lapse approach bears comparison to Rineke Dijkstra's projects *Oliver Silva* (2000 – 2002) and *Almerisa* (1994 – 2003), which chart respectively the development of a young French Foreign Legionnaire, and an East European immigrant to the Netherlands. Both series, as Gil Blank has observed, hinge on subjects who have surrendered, and then reconstructed, their identities.[4] Blake's portraits of adolescents offer similar reflections of still-unformed identities, as they shift and are shaped by personal drives and desires, against the larger social structures of family, school, and the sporting world. There are hints of incongruity between the 'official' sporting persona dressed in regulation kit, and the hairstyles, make-up and jewellery that indicate fashion allegiance or personal taste. This is perhaps most succinctly expressed in a profile portrait of Curtis Miller, whose flamboyant diamond ear-stud defiantly contrasts with the formality of his fencing jacket.

Whilst Dijkstra's *Oliver Silva* and *Almerisa* seem to depict identities that are rendered 'blank slates', the subjects of Blake's portraits demonstrate greater agency. They may be swayed by the pressures of school, parents, and sporting bodies, but what impresses the viewer is their personal drive as they negotiate these constraints. This is partly due to Blake's decision to display the images alongside excerpts from texts the young people have written at his request. Occasionally naïve or overblown, but often movingly honest, their words offer insights into their doubts, fears, and resilience during their often solitary career. It is through these words that we become aware of the psychological strength of character needed by these athletes to succeed.

Perhaps some of the most charged demonstrations of power come from the fencing arena. In these portraits, the subjects are literally armoured from our gaze. A striking image of Alex Craig shows her face barely perceptible through the mesh of the mask, described by her as 'mental protection from piercing thoughts'. A close-up of Ayesha Fihosy shows her mask pushed to the top of her head, like a helmet, as she meets the camera with an uncompromising stare. In this image and those of her peer Curtis Miller, we might reflect on how the colonising gaze of ethnographic photography is turned on itself. Here, Blake (himself a mixed-race Briton) depicts the two powerful fencers attired in the garb of a sport once reserved for white European aristocrats, as they compete to take their place on the national team.

Blake is also sensitive to the power dynamics of depicting adolescents. The recent trend in art photography for images of teenagers has been criticised as potentially sexually exploitative: Joanne Woodall describes Hellen van Meene's photography of young girls as 'a kind of defloration'.[5] By contrast, Blake's adolescents do not seem hesitant or vulnerable before our gaze. Swimmers Sophie Allen and Rosie Bancroft, despite wearing only swimsuits, do not appear awkwardly naked. Perhaps used to their bodies being appraised as functional mechanisms, assessed on power rather than looks, they exhibit a kind of confidence in their poses. That is not to say they appear entirely without introspection and doubts, but their bodies do not seem so painfully exposed. Blake's images of Bancroft, who wears a prosthesis due to amputation just below her knee, are particularly compelling. Neither embarrassed nor defiant, Bancroft's understated composure is highly moving.

Blake's restrained and subtle portraits offer a welcome alternative to those conventional images of sport that emphasise action and overt emotion. His complex portrayals bear repeated viewing and will continue to reward the onlooker long after London 2012 is over. Perhaps one of his most interesting contributions is the way in which his young subjects refuse to be seen simply in terms of fashion or sexual desirability. They are not models and are sometimes physically flawed in terms of Western commercialised standards of beauty. Instead, their bodies are honed as tools of sporting prowess, rather than as objects to be viewed. As the subjects' writings make clear, their ambition goes beyond the desire to simply achieve external approval. Ultimately, they are driven by the need to overcome their self-doubt, to challenge their own limits, and achieve their personal best.

Pippa Oldfield is the Head of Programme, Impressions Gallery, Bradford, and a Doctoral Fellow at Durham University.

1. Peter Skinner, *Sports Photography: How to Capture Action and Emotion* (New York: Allworth Press, 2007)

2. For an overview of the visual culture of sport more generally, see Mike Huggins, 'The Sporting Gaze: Towards a Visual Turn in Sports History – Documenting Art and Sport', in *Journal of Sport History*, Vol. 35, No.2 (2008), pp.311–329

3. Julian Stallabrass, 'What's in a Face? Blankness and Significance in Contemporary Art Photography', *October* 122 (2007), pp.71–90

4. Gil Blank, 'What Does a Portrait, Human and Unsentimental, Look Like Now?', *Influence*, No. 2 (2004), pp.76–89

5. Joanne Woodall, 'At the Threshold' in *The Citibank Private Bank Photography Prize 2001*, (London: The Photographers Gallery, 2001), pp.45–57

Every part of me was shaking. My teeth were chattering, even though it was hot. I felt sick. I fidgeted, pulling the zipper up and down on my jacket. Why am I this nervous? I had done this race millions of times before. But no matter what I did, this fear was there. I took a huge gasp of breath and blew out slowly as I stood up to my block.

The only other time fear had taken over me was a few months before in a very different situation… everywhere was bright. Bright walls, bright lights, bright beds. I was half listening to the bubbly nurse telling me about eating and anaesthetic and pain relief. Then another girl went wheeling past in a hospital bed, drips and needles attached to her arm. My heart started pounding, I started to feel sick. I knew that this operation was the best thing. But I still wanted more than anything for it not to happen.

I put my hands over the edge of the block and looked in to the water. Oh god, FOCUS. In a flash I was in the water, frantically pulling as much water past me as I could, kicking my legs, doing what came so naturally to me. My heart pounded. Adrenaline threw me forward, but it was hard; the girl next to me was ahead by at least a body length, the spectators cheering, my coach shouting. I saw the wall ahead of me and gasped in air before plunging in to a turn, legs flipping, head spinning. I was off again. Halfway there, halfway there, I thought.

The few months after my operation were ones of extreme pain, loneliness and desperation. Being in one room for several weeks, not able to walk, shower or do anything for yourself. Next came the painfully slow journey back to normality.

My lungs were burning, my muscles ached and my chest hurt, gasping for breath at any possible chance. I started to fade, as the pain and ache from my muscles started to win. I fought back. 5 metres of pool left before the wall. This is it. I sucked in one last breath and threw myself forward.

The first time I swum after surgery was in the hydro-pool at the hospital. Part of me couldn't wait to get in. But another part was terrified, what if I hurt my leg? What if it gets infected? What if I can't even swim anymore? I got in. It felt like it was the first time my leg had ever felt water, but I could swim! It was amazing.

I didn't breathe in those last few metres. I put my head down and sprinted, giving every last bit of me. I felt the rough wall as I smashed my hand into it, lifting my head out to gasp in air. I frantically searched the board. Second. I couldn't believe it, it was a national competition and my very first race since my operations. And I came second. I searched for my mum's face in the crowd and saw her pumping her fist in the air, tears rolling down her cheeks.

It had been a very long, slow journey to get to that moment. Going back to training was very scary, and very hard. Although I had swum right through the summer whilst everyone else was on holidays I still had missed 3 months of training. Standing on the podium for my silver medal, I was so emotional. It wasn't the best time I'd ever swum, I didn't swim it with perfect technique or pacing, it didn't qualify me for any major competition or programme and it didn't break a record or make history. But it was one of my best ever races because I showed that all the set backs I had faced were not going to stop me. I'll give everything I have, to achieve my dream.

Rosie Bancroft is currently training as part of UK Sports World Class Talent programme.

Rosie Bancroft | *Swimming* | 2007

Rosie Bancroft | *Swimming* | 2008

Standing on the podium for my silver medal, I was so emotional. It wasn't the best time I'd ever swum, I didn't swim it with perfect technique or pacing, it didn't qualify me for any major competition or programme and it didn't break a record or make history. But it was one of my best ever races because I showed that all the set backs I had faced were not going to stop me.

Rosie Bancroft | *Swimming* | 2011

Robert Jeffries | *Kayaking* | 2007

It becomes an addiction every time I arrive at a river. The amount of concentration required is so much that I often don't hear people cheering on the banks as I put everything into nailing the right line through the water.

Robert Jeffries | *Kayaking* | 2009

Robert Jeffries | *Kayaking* | 2010

The mask is like a window into a different world. It is there when you need it to hide tears of frustration or just to retain focus for the next bout. It allows me to leave things behind. The wire mesh is for my physical protection, but it gives me mental protection too from my penetrating thoughts.

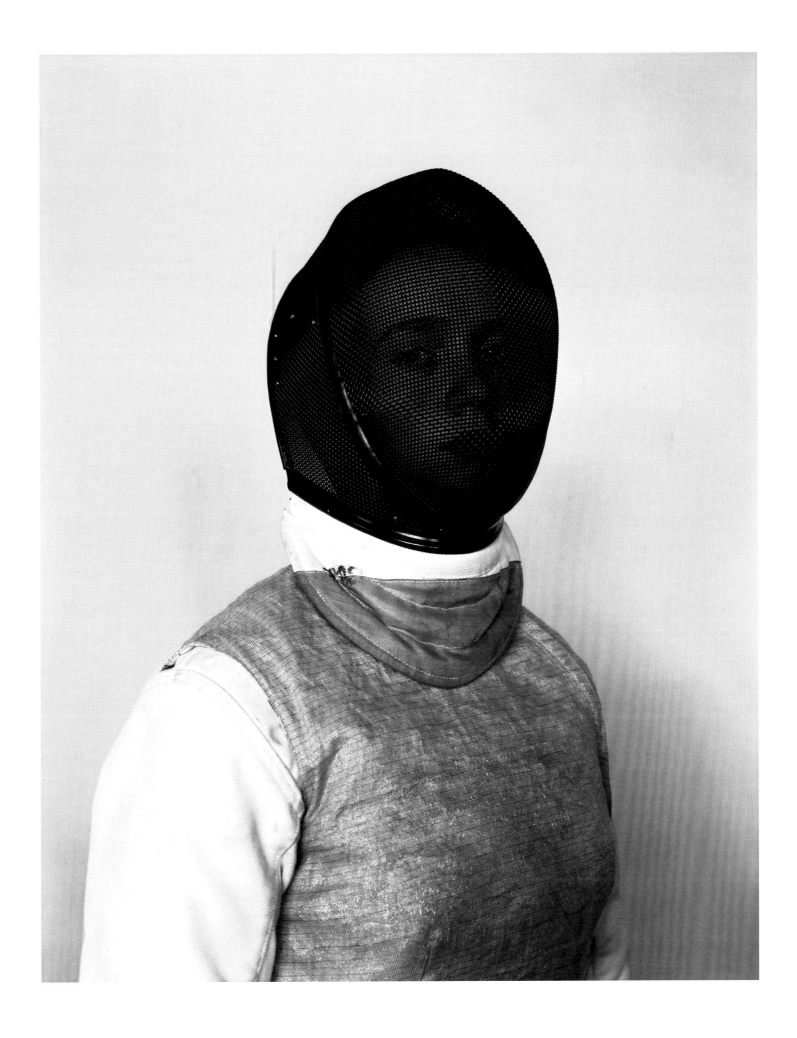

Alex Craig | *Fencing* | 2011

Kelly Ann Downey | *Judo* | 2007

Kelly Ann Downey | *Judo* | 2008

After all the years I put into Welsh judo, they took my funding and treated me and my feelings disgustingly, so I decided to leave the sport I loved. My parents had done so much for me when I was competing but they didn't handle my decision to quit very well at first. They're having a blast now, going on holidays, treating themselves and enjoying life, and I'm proud to have just finished college with a triple distinction in sports development.

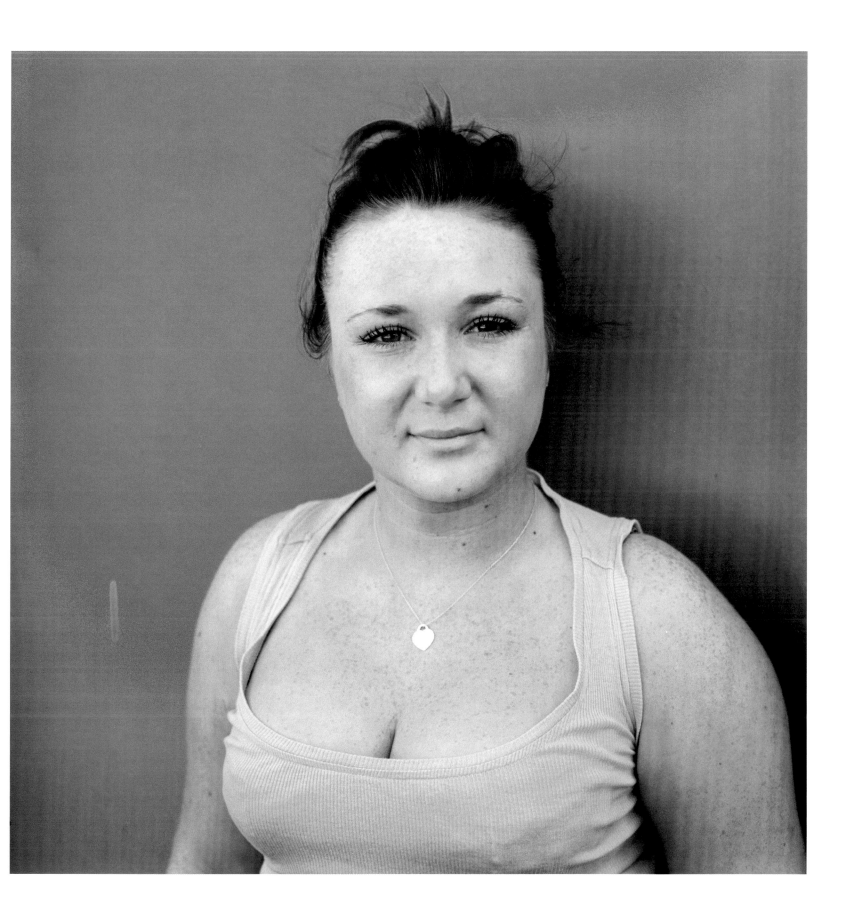

Ashley Facey Thompson | *Table Tennis* | 2011

Ayesha Fihosy | *Fencing* | 2010

Ayesha Fihosy | *Fencing* | 2010

The costs of kit/equipment, club fees/coaching, international and domestic competitions and fencing camps are becoming unaffordable. It's a very sad subject for me to talk about. It would be tragic if I had to give up after everything I have put into it.

This sport makes me creak and ache prematurely and experience pain during training and races. If I am hurting I try to make myself hurt more. I try to get to the stage where I cannot run one more step at the end, where I cannot even stand up because then I know I have given my all. Despite the daily soreness, early mornings, calorie counting and to some extent loss of a 'normal' teenage life, I keep going back for more.

Rosie Edwards | *Marathon* | 2007

Rosie Edwards | *Marathon* | 2008

Rosie Edwards | *Marathon* | 2011

Matt Roberts | *High Jump* | 2007

Matt Roberts | *High Jump* | 2010

The self inflicted aches and pains, the burn of exhausted muscles, testosterone releases and other self induced highs. Crushing doubts and negativity, bigger enemies than rivals will ever be.

Sam Ridley | *Fencing* | 2008

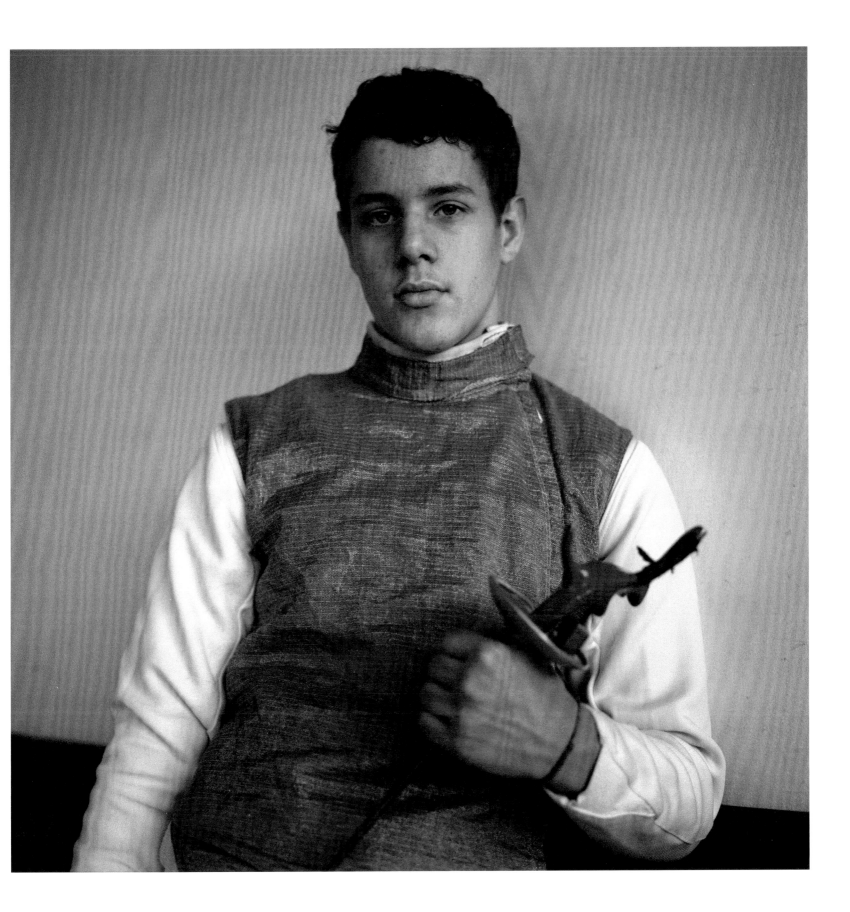

I should have won my first two fights quite easily in theory, but was beaten 14–15 in both. My frustration was taken out on a wall followed by five hours in a German hospital. This moment of madness caused me to miss the European Championships in Athens which was one of my goals for 2010.

Sam Ridley | *Fencing* | 2010

Helen Dunning | *3 Day Eventing* | 2007

Helen Dunning | *3 Day Eventing* | 2008

If you have a strong relationship with your horse and trust their talent and your ability, nerves just become a part of wanting to win and determination takes over. But without a fabulous owner and my support team of vets, farriers, trainers, parents and sponsors I wouldn't be able to carry on.

Helen Dunning | *3 Day Eventing* | 2009

Over the years I've had to create an alternate personality. Outside the ring I am a lively bubbly person always looking for the positives. But once I step onto the mat to fight, my alternate personality takes over. The movement, attitude and aggression that I bring is unbelievable at times, even for me.

Amin Badr | *Taekwondo* | 2010

Brandon Tutthill | *Judo* | 2008

Brandon Tutthill | *Judo* | 2009

Brandon Tutthill | *Judo* | 2011

Lucy Davidson | *Table Tennis* | 2007

Lucy Davidson | *Table Tennis* | 2009

Lucy Davidson | *Table Tennis* | 2009

70% of our funding got cut, because the government felt that other sports had more chance to win medals at the Olympics than us. I went from being one of the top girl table tennis players in Britain, to feeling like someone had thrown me on the floor and stamped on me. I sacrificed my education, life, friends and money for it all to be thrown back in my face. I don't deserve it, so I said enough is enough.

Curtis Miller | *Fencing* | 2010

Curtis Miller | *Fencing* | 2011

Gabby White | *Badminton* | 2007

Gabby White | *Badminton* | 2009

Gabby White | *Badminton* | 2010

Sophie Allen | *Swimming* | 2007

Sophie Allen | *Swimming* | 2008

This was the event to qualify for the worlds but after twelve months injury and rehabilitation it would take something special to get my confidence back. When I hit the wall in second place, only 0.1 seconds shy of my best time before my operation; it felt amazing! But in the end I was devastated to find I was still 0.7 seconds off the qualifying time.

When sport makes it from the back pages to the front in the press, it might be for some outrage or for some good news story about improving health (especially combatting obesity), reducing crime, personal development, improving educational performance or promoting community cohesion. In public/political arenas I have been known to advance similar cases regarding social benefit; in academic circles I am more likely to question where the substantiating evidence is for these benefits. After all, in addition to being a force for good, sport may foster racism, sexism, homophobia, cheating, disrespect for others… Jingoistic tub thumping does a disservice to those seeking to maximise what sport may deliver for society. A more rounded and complex appreciation is essential, and that can be supported by recognising diversity of experience as demonstrated here.

One of the hopes for London 2012 has been that it should ignite a passion for sport such that more people should be moved to participate – Lord Coe has frequently recounted the effect watching John Sherwood's performance in the Mexico Olympics of 1968 had on the young Seb. Targets were set for a mass participation legacy from London 2012. Unfortunately, adult participation has steadfastly refused to make any significant move upwards. However, Sport England's *Sport Unlimited* initiative, co-ordinated by the County Sports Partnerships across the country, has been claiming considerable success among young people. By providing opportunities for those in secondary education to get involved beyond school, the project evaluation suggests some 1.2 million young people took part in its sporting activities; more importantly, many reported continuing their participation in sport after the end of the project. Now slimmed down and rebranded as *Sportivate* its target has shifted to the 14 to 25 age group to try to prevent people dropping out of sport in their teens and early adulthood.

The sport photographs we are most familiar with are those that represent either achievement in action (goal/try-scoring or the cross-court winner) or achievement in celebration (somersaults, punching the air, parading the trophy). The portraits here represent achievement in reflection.

Those who became involved in this photographic project 5 years ago were already much more deeply engaged than the *Sportivate* participants. Their involvement was the kind that requires not just skill, but the commitment to devote large amounts of time to improving their performance (thereby not being able to do a range of other activities) and the resilience to deal with setbacks. We know from research the importance of the support package from schools, clubs and coaches, but particularly from family and friends, something that can be appreciated from some of the accompanying accounts here.

Even without those stories the photographs would offer engaging narratives. Each photograph tells its own story, but unusually, perhaps uniquely, here we have sequences of photographs that tell a development tale as the athletes grow into their sport. As had to be expected some of those sequences were brought to an end before 2012. The convention of telling the stories of ultimate sporting success, makes it all the more important to consider the journeys that appeared to be heading in the same direction and then were interrupted. The narrative processes involved in creating and sharing stories of one's life are an important way of people claiming their identity; through that process we can start to define who we are, who we were, and where we may be in the future. Those stories then help people 'make sense' of their experiences in relation to the (sporting) context in which they are immersed, hence the importance of supporting young people in telling their stories and the need for others to take seriously the stories that arise. If others are prepared to hear the voices of young athletes it should help both keep their interest and stimulate their performance.

The academic literature is replete with semiotic analyses trying to 'deconstruct' the image and ascribe meaning. It's a good game. For me the importance of these photographs is that they invite us to consider the back stories, contemplate the person behind the performer and the everyday aspects of their lives not just the medal podium or its equivalent.

With this collection the photographer has ceded a lot of the power that photographers normally retain for themselves in directing every stage of the process. These are not just photographs of athletes, but pictures that they have had a part in constructing and then providing the accompanying text so that they can have a say in how they are presented to the world. Some of the photographs suggest the composure so important for successful athletes; others portray the drained feeling that often follows the competition high. To appreciate some of the wider array of emotions further, we can look to the text provided by the athletes themselves. One talks about the actual mask that not only protects her from the fencing foil, but from the scrutiny of others too. Others talk about the symbolic mask they assume when entering the sporting arena in order to shut everything else out.

Seeing people's images and reading their stories not only allows us to analyse their achievement, but invites us to consider our own. Given the talent, how many of us would have chosen the extraordinarily focused path that is expected of those setting their sights on being the best in their sport? On reflection most of us would probably think it would not be for us, but on further reflection still there may be others who have been similarly single-minded in their own careers. The photographs in this collection not only reflect the personal best of the young sports men and women involved, but also what Paul Floyd Blake has selected as his personal best.

Professor Jonathan Long, Carnegie Research Institute,
Leeds Metropolitan University.

Most of the athletes featured in this book were introduced to the photographer by the UK sports charity SportsAid. SportsAid plays an important role in the British sports industry, finding and funding the next generation of champions by giving promising young athletes financial support during their formative years – when training is competing with schoolwork and mum and dad are picking up the bills.

Established in 1976, the charity now makes around 2,000 awards to young sportsmen and women throughout the UK each year, most of whom are aged 12 to 20. With the average cost of pursuing a top-level, junior sports career at around £5,500 a year, the need to help these athletes stay in sport and be able to compete at their best is an essential part of British sport's talent pathway.

As the 2008 Olympic and Paralympic Games in Beijing showed, the impact of helping them is considerable. That year, more than a third of Britain's 42 Paralympic gold medals and 18 of Britain's 19 Olympic gold medals went to people who have received support from SportsAid.

www.sportsaid.org.uk

Biography

Paul Floyd Blake is a mixed race, Jamaican-English photographer, who started his professional career in photography in 2001, following many years working as a lorry driver, and as a semi-professional footballer.

Blake focuses on the intricacies of ordinary life, using a mixture of portraiture and landscape that blend classical compositions with contemporary issues. His themes are the new cultures and identities born out of an era in which we are no longer defined purely by our race or class, but have multiple identities that change according to environment and context.

Blake's work has been shown in solo exhibitions at Manchester Art Gallery; Gallery Oldham; Piece Hall Gallery, Halifax; Impressions Gallery, Bradford; and Folly Gallery, Lancaster. In addition, he has exhibited widely in group shows including *The Human Game*, Foundazione Pitti, Florence; *Aftershock*, Commonwealth Games Manchester, Zion Arts Centre; *Ways of Looking* photography festival, Bradford; Sports Lab, Weston Park, Sheffield; the Victoria and Albert Museum of Childhood, London; and *The World in London*, The Photographers Gallery, London.

His portrait of Rosie Bancroft was overall winner of the prestigious Taylor Wessing Photographic Portrait Prize 2009, and exhibited at the National Portrait Gallery, London. Blake also undertakes regular commissions for the *Telegraph Magazine*, *Times Educational Supplement*, and Arts Council England, amongst others.

Thank you

The author would like to thank Professor Jonathan Long and Pippa Oldfield for the generous words they have contributed; Arts Council England for financial support with the project, and Dewi Lewis for publishing this book. In addition the book would not have been possible without the help of Anne McNeill and Pippa Oldfield from Impressions Gallery, Bradford, and their support throughout the development of this project; Patrick Henry of Open Eye Gallery and the photographer Julian Germain, for their advice over many years; James Corazzo for his excellent design work on this book. I don't know how he did it alongside a new job and new baby. Thank you so much. Simon Ford for the hours he spent scanning and colour balancing the images and Michael Lomax for spotting them. Special thanks to my partner Leila Jancovich for putting up with my stress. Thanks to Harry Pearson for his feedback on the work.

Above all thanks go to all the athletes and their families for collaborating in this project; to those who wrote about their experiences and in particular to Rosie Bancroft for allowing me to use her story in full. It has been fantastic for me to share in your experiences over the last 5 years. I wish you all the very best in whatever you do from here.

First published in the UK by

Dewi Lewis Publishing
8 Broomfield Road, Heaton Moor
Stockport SK4 4ND, England
www.dewilewispublishing.com

in association with
Impressions Gallery
Centenary Square
Bradford BD1 1SD
www.impressions-gallery.com

Published to coincide with London
2012 Olympic and Paralympic Games
and a solo exhibition at
Impressions Gallery
29 June – 8 September 2012

ISBN: 978-1-907893-21-6

Design: James Corazzo, www.corazzo.eu
Editorial advice: Pippa Oldfield
Production: Dewi Lewis Publishing
Print: EBS, Verona, Italy

LOTTERY FUNDED   SportsAid   impressionsgallery